A Creamy Soup Cookbook

A Soup Cookbook Filled with Delicious Soup Recipes for Those Who Love Creamy Soups

By
BookSumo Press
All rights reserved

Published by
http://www.booksumo.com

Table of Contents

Wild Hollandaise Crab Soup 4
Asparagus and Soy Cream Soup 5
Classic Soup Cream 6
Light Thyme Mushroom Soup 7
Rosemary Gnocchi Soup 8
Creamy Carrot and celery Curry Soup 9
Spinach Cream 10
Potato Flakes Soup 11
Chunky Asparagus Soup 12
Chicken and Celery Cream Soup 13
Swiss Cauliflower Soup 14
Cauliflower Cream Curry 15
Healing Spring Soup 16
Chicken Flavored Broccoli Soup 17
Chilled Summer Mango Soup 18
Italian Basil Tomato Soup 19
Artichoke Soup 20
Bell Cheese Soup 21
Roasted Halloween Soup 22
Cheesy Turkey Soup 23
Cheesy Green Florets Soup 24
Spicy Loaded Elk Soup 25
Creamy Gorgonzola Soup 26
Dill Soup 27
Creamy Masala Quinoa Soup 28
Creamy Pumpkin Asiago Soup 29
Classic Creamy Potato Soup 30
Chunky Chicken and Lemon Soup 31

Worcestershire Cheddar Soup 32
Creamy Bacon Soup 33
Chilled Creamy Dill Soup 34
Limy Corn Soup 35
Fancy Asparagus Cream 36
Hot Cheese Soup 37
Jerusalem Chicken Soup 38
Chunky Milk Soup 39
Herbed Chicken Soup 40
Apple Cider Beef Soup 41
Baked Spears Soup Casserole 42
Pesto Topping Soup 43
Old Bay's Creamy Crab Soup 44
Anti-Vampires Soup 45
Cheesy Parsley Flowers Soup 46
Alaskan Broth Soup 47
Twisted Onion Soup 48
Creamy Mozzarella Soup 49
Classic Tomato Soup 50
Festive Sweet and Salty Pumpkin Soup 51
Creamy Sausage Mushroom Soup 52
Homemade Chicken and Mushroom Cream Soup 53

WILD HOLLANDAISE
Crab Soup

🥣 Prep Time: 15 mins
🕐 Total Time: 45 mins

Servings per Recipe: 6
Calories   543 kcal
Fat   45.2 g
Carbohydrates   15.3g
Protein   20.4 g
Cholesterol   188 mg
Sodium   1447 mg

Ingredients

3 tbsp all-purpose flour
1 (1.25 oz) envelope hollandaise sauce mix
4 C. half-and-half, divided
1/4 C. butter
3 tbsp Old Bay Seasoning TM

1/2 tsp dry mustard
1/4 tsp celery seed
1 C. whipping cream
1 tbsp apple cider
1 lb fresh crabmeat

Directions

1. Get a mixing bowl: Add the flour and hollandaise sauce mix with 2 C. half-and-half then mix them well.
2. Place a large saucepan over medium heat. Melt the butter in it. Stir in the flour mix until it thickens.
3. Stir in the rest of the half and half, Old Bay, dry mustard, celery seed, and whipping cream.
4. Cook the mix until it starts summering. Lower the heat and stir in the crabmeat with apple cider.
5. Cook the soup until it is heated through while stirring all the time. Adjust the seasoning of the soup and serve it right away.
6. Enjoy.

Asparagus and Soy Cream Soup

Prep Time: 30 mins
Total Time: 1 hr

Servings per Recipe: 6
Calories   211 kcal
Fat   12.5 g
Carbohydrates   18.3g
Protein   8 g
Cholesterol   14 mg
Sodium   2019 mg

Ingredients

- 1/4 C. margarine
- 1 onion, chopped
- 3 stalks celery, chopped
- 3 tbsp all-purpose flour
- 4 C. water
- 1 (10.5 oz) can condensed chicken broth
- 4 tbsp chicken bouillon powder
- 1 potato, peeled and diced
- 1 lb fresh asparagus, trimmed and coarsely chopped
- 3/4 C. half-and-half
- 1 tbsp soy sauce
- 1/4 tsp ground black pepper
- 1/4 tsp ground white pepper

Directions

1. Place a medium pot over medium heat. Cook in it the butter until it melts. Cook in it the onions and chopped celery for 5 min.
2. Add the flour and stir them then let them cook for 2 min while mixing them all the time. Stir in the water, chicken broth, and chicken soup base until they become creamy.
3. Stir in the asparagus with potato. Lower the heat and bring the soup to a simmer. Cook the soup for 22 min.
4. Get a food processor: Allow the soup to cool down slightly then transfer it to the food processor. Blend the soup until it becomes creamy.
5. Pour the soup back into the pot. Add the half and half cream, soy sauce, and black and white pepper.
6. Cook the soup until it starts boiling. Serve your soup warm.
7. Enjoy.

CLASSIC
Soup Cream

🍲 Prep Time: 15 mins
🕐 Total Time: 15 mins

Servings per Recipe: 8
Calories 156 kcal
Fat 12.8 g
Carbohydrates 7.6g
Protein 2.9 g
Cholesterol 36 mg
Sodium 395 mg

Ingredients

1/2 C. butter
6 tbsp all-purpose flour
2 C. milk

2 cubes chicken bouillon
Ground black pepper to taste

Directions

1. Place a large saucepan over medium heat. Cook the butter in it until it melts. Stir in the milk and bouillon cubes.
2. Lower the heat and simmer the soup until it becomes thick. Stir in your favorite veggies, cheese or any other
3. Ingredients
4. Adjust the seasoning of the soup then serve it warm.
5. Enjoy.

Light Thyme Mushroom Soup

> Prep Time: 15 mins
> Total Time: 30 mins
>
> Servings per Recipe: 4
> Calories   295 kcal
> Fat   23.8 g
> Carbohydrates   16 g
> Protein   7.1 g
> Cholesterol   40 mg
> Sodium   624 mg

Ingredients

- 1 lb fresh mushrooms
- 1/4 C. margarine
- 4 green onions, thinly sliced
- 3 cloves garlic, chopped
- 1 tsp chopped fresh thyme
- 2 tbsp all-purpose flour
- 4 C. vegetable broth
- 1 C. light cream
- Salt and pepper to taste
- 1 sprig fresh thyme leaves
- 1 tbsp chopped fresh chives

Directions

1. Remove the mushroom stalks and slice them.
2. Place a large saucepan over medium heat. Add the butter and cook it until it melts. Add the onion, garlic and lemon thyme. Cook them for 2 min.
3. Stir in the mushroom and salt and white pepper. Cook them for 5 min. Stir in the flour and mix them for 1 min.
4. Turn off the heat and stir in the stock until they are well combined. Turn on the heat to medium and bring the soup to a boil then lower the heat and cook it for 3 min while stirring it often.
5. Stir in the cream until it is well combined. Adjust the seasoning of the soup then serve it warm.
6. Enjoy

ROSEMARY GNOCCHI
Soup

🥣 Prep Time: 20 mins
🕐 Total Time: 45 mins

Servings per Recipe: 8
Calories 311 kcal
Fat 20.6 g
Carbohydrates 19.7g
Protein 11.7 g
Cholesterol 43 mg
Sodium 854 mg

Ingredients

- 1/2 C. margarine
- 3/4 C. finely chopped onion
- 3/4 C. finely chopped celery
- 1/2 C. finely grated carrot
- 1 1/2 tsp minced garlic
- 1/3 C. all-purpose flour
- 4 C. chicken broth
- 3/4 C. half-and-half
- 3/4 C. milk
- 1 (16 oz) package potato gnocchi
- 1 1/2 C. chopped cooked chicken
- 3/4 C. shredded fresh spinach
- 1/2 tsp dried rosemary
- 1/2 tsp salt
- 1/4 tsp ground black pepper
- 1/4 tsp allspice

Directions

1. Place a large saucepan over medium heat. Add the butter and melt it. Cook in it the onion, celery, carrot, and garlic for 8 min.
2. Stir in the flour and mix them well while cooking them for 5 min.
3. Add the chicken broth, half-and-half, and milk then bring them to a rolling boil. Lower the heat and add the gnocchi, chicken, and spinach, rosemary, salt, black pepper, and allspice.
4. Simmer the soup for 9 min. Adjust the seasoning of the soup then serve it warm.
5. Enjoy.

Creamy Carrot and celery Curry Soup

Prep Time: 20 mins
Total Time: 1 hr 15 mins

Servings per Recipe: 8
Calories   169 kcal
Fat   11.7 g
Carbohydrates   14.8 g
Protein   2.3 g
Cholesterol   38 mg
Sodium   586 mg

Ingredients

- 1/4 C. butter, cubed
- 2 1/2 C. sliced carrots
- 1 large potato, peeled and cubed
- 1 C. chopped onion
- 1 stalk celery, chopped
- 3 C. chicken broth
- 1 tsp ground ginger
- 1/2 C. heavy whipping cream
- 1 tsp curry powder
- 1/2 tsp salt
- 1/8 tsp ground black pepper

Directions

1. Place a large soup over medium heat. Add the butter and melt it in it. Stir in the carrots, potato, onion, celery, chicken broth, and ginger.
2. Put on the lid and lower the heat then simmer the soup for 34 min. Remove the lid and turn off the heat then allow the soup lose heat for 15 min.
3. Get a food processor: Use it to blend the soup in parts until it becomes creamy. Pour the soup back into the pot then stir into it the rest of the
4. Ingredients
5. Simmer the soup on low heat for 12 min. Adjust the seasoning of the soup then serve it warm.
6. Enjoy.

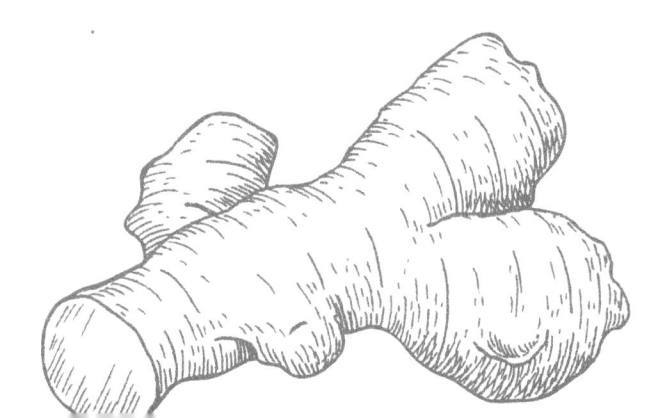

SPINACH
Cream

🥣 Prep Time: 5 mins
🕐 Total Time: 25 mins

Servings per Recipe: 4
Calories	227 kcal
Fat	12.9 g
Carbohydrates	19.1g
Protein	10.1 g
Cholesterol	38 mg
Sodium	1053 mg

Ingredients

- 1 1/2 C. water
- 3 cubes chicken bouillon
- 1 (10 oz) package frozen chopped spinach
- 3 tbsp butter
- 1/4 C. all-purpose flour
- 3 C. milk
- 1 tbsp dried minced onion
- Salt and pepper to taste

Directions

1. Place a heavy saucepan over medium heat. Add the water, bouillon, and spinach then cook them until they start boiling.
2. Place a saucepan over medium heat. Add the butter and melt it. Add the flour and mix them well while cooking them for 2 min.
3. Drizzle the milk on them gradually while whisking all the time until they become smooth and cream.
4. Add the minced onion, salt, and pepper then stir them for 5 min on low heat until they thicken. Stir in the spinach mix and simmer them for 2 min.
5. Adjust the seasoning of the soup then serve it warm.
6. Enjoy.

Potato Flakes Soup

🍲 Prep Time: 15 mins
🕐 Total Time: 55 mins

Servings per Recipe: 8
Calories   307 kcal
Fat   14.2 g
Carbohydrates   34.3g
Protein   10.7 g
Cholesterol   25 mg
Sodium   773 mg

Ingredients

6 slices turkey bacon, diced
1 onion, chopped
1 tbsp all-purpose flour
6 C. chicken broth

6 potatoes, thinly sliced
1/2 C. instant mashed potato flakes
1 C. half-and-half

Directions

1. Cook the bacon in a large skillet with onion for 6 min then drain then place them aside.
2. Cook the flour for 1 min in a large saucepan then drizzle on it the broth while stirring all the time. Cook them until they start boiling.
3. Add the cooked onion mix with the potatoes, a pinch of salt and pepper. Lower the heat and put on the lid then cook the soup for 35 min.
4. Adjust the seasoning of the soup then serve it warm.
5. Enjoy.

CHUNKY ASPARAGUS
Soup

Prep Time: 15 mins
Total Time: 55 mins

Servings per Recipe: 8
Calories	182 kcal
Fat	12.1 g
Carbohydrates	13.5g
Protein	5.9 g
Cholesterol	33 mg
Sodium	867 mg

Ingredients

- 3 slices turkey bacon
- 1 tbsp turkey bacon drippings
- 1/4 C. butter
- 3 stalks celery, chopped
- 1 onion, diced
- 3 tbsp all-purpose flour
- 6 C. chicken broth
- 1 potato, peeled and diced
- 1 lb fresh asparagus, tips set aside and stalks chopped
- Salt and ground black pepper to taste
- 1 (8 oz) package sliced fresh mushrooms
- 3/4 C. half-and-half cream

Directions

1. Place a large pan over medium heat. Cook in it the bacon slices until they become crispy then drain them and place it aside to drain. Reserve 1 tbsp of bacon grease.
2. Place a large saucepan over medium heat. Melt in the bacon grease with butter. Add the celery with onion and cook them for 5 min.
3. Mix in the flour and cook them for 2 min. add the chicken broth gradually while stirring all the time. Cook the soup until it starts boiling.
4. Stir in the asparagus stalks with potato, a pinch of salt and pepper. Lower the heat and put on the lid. Cook the soup for 22 min. allow the soup to cool down for 10 min.
5. Get a food processor: Add the soup in batches and blend it smooth then pour it back into the pot.
6. Cook the asparagus tips with mushroom, a pinch of salt and pepper in the pan where you cooked the bacon. Cook them for 7 min.
7. Add the mushroom mix half and half to the soup and bring it to a boil. Crumble the bacon and serve it with the soup as a topping.
8. Enjoy.

Chicken and Celery Cream Soup

Prep Time: 20 mins
Total Time: 40 mins

Servings per Recipe: 32
Calories   126 kcal
Fat   7.8 g
Carbohydrates 10.3g
Protein   4.1 g
Cholesterol   8 mg
Sodium   615 mg

Ingredients

3 quarts chicken stock
3 lb celery, coarsely chopped
1/2 lb carrots, julienned
1/2 lb onions, chopped
1 C. all-purpose flour
1 tbsp salt
1 tsp ground white pepper
3 quarts hot milk
1 C. margarine

Directions

1. Place a large pot over medium heat. Add the stock and cook it until it starts boiling. Stir in the carrot with celery and onion.
2. Get a small mixing bowl: Add the flour, salt, pepper, and milk. Mix them well. Stir the mix into the broth with margarine.
3. Cook the soup until it starts boiling. Keep boiling the soup for 12 min. Drain the veggies and place them aside for another use. Adjust the seasoning of the soup then serve it warm.
4. Enjoy.

SWISS CAULIFLOWER
Soup

🍲 Prep Time: 20 mins
⏱ Total Time: 40 mins

Servings per Recipe: 12
Calories   256 kcal
Fat   18.9 g
Carbohydrates   10.3g
Protein   8.7 g
Cholesterol   62 mg
Sodium   81 mg

Ingredients

5 tbsp unsalted butter
1 leek, chopped
1 onion, chopped
1 carrot, chopped
1 tsp dried tarragon
1/2 tsp dried thyme
1/4 C. all-purpose flour
1 C. vegtable broth
6 C. chicken stock

Salt to taste
1/4 tsp freshly ground white pepper
1 head cauliflower, broken into small florets
1 C. milk
1 C. heavy whipping cream
2 1/2 C. shredded Swiss cheese (optional)

Directions

1. Bring a salted pot of water to a boil. Place on it a steamer and cook in it the cauliflower until it becomes tender.
2. Place a large pot over medium heat. Cook in the margarine until it melts. Add the leek, onion, and carrot then cook them for 12 min.
3. Add the thyme with tarragon and cook them for 2 min. Stir in the flour for 1 min. Lower the heat and add the stock with broth, a pinch of salt and pepper.
4. Stir in the cauliflower and bring the soup to a simmer. Remove the lid and cook the soup over low heat for 32 min.
5. Get a food processor: Allow the soup to cool down for 10 min. blend the soup in batches in the food processor until it becomes smooth and creamy.
6. Pour the soup back into the pot. Add the cream with milk and cook the soup for 5 min. Stir in the cheese until it melts.
7. Adjust the seasoning of the soup then serve it warm.
8. Enjoy.

Cauliflower Cream Curry

> Prep Time: 15 mins
> Total Time: 1 hr 5 mins

Servings per Recipe: 4
Calories   359 kcal
Fat   32.7 g
Carbohydrates   15.1g
Protein   5.4 g
Cholesterol   90 mg
Sodium   1391 mg

Ingredients

- 1 head cauliflower, cut into florets
- 2 tbsp vegetable oil
- 1 tsp salt
- 1 tbsp butter, cut into small pieces
- 1 large yellow onion, diced
- 1 tsp chopped garlic
- 1 tsp curry powder
- 1 tsp cayenne pepper
- 1 tsp ground turmeric
- 1 quart chicken stock
- 1 C. heavy whipping cream
- Salt and ground black pepper to taste
- 2 tbsp chopped fresh parsley

Directions

1. Before you do anything set the oven to 450 F.
2. Combine the cauliflower florets with vegetable oil and 1 tsp in a large mixing bowl. Place the mix on a lined up baking pan.
3. Cook the cauliflower in the oven for 28 min while stirring it every 10 min.
4. Place a large saucepan over medium heat. Add the butter and cook it until it melts. Cook in it the onion for 6 min. add the garlic and cook them for 3 min.
5. Stir in the curry powder, cayenne pepper, and ground turmeric. Cook them for 6 min while stirring them often.
6. Add the stock with cooked cauliflower. Cook them until they start boiling. Remove the lid and lower the heat. Cook the soup for 12 min.
7. Get a food processor: Allow the soup to cool down for 10 min. blend the soup in batches in the food processor until it becomes smooth and creamy.
8. Pour the soup back into the pot. Add the cream with a pinch of salt and pepper then cook it for 5 min.
9. Adjust the seasoning of the soup then serve it warm.
10. Enjoy.

HEALING SPRING Soup

Prep Time: 15 mins
Total Time: 1 hr

Servings per Recipe: 8
Calories   127 kcal
Fat   9.8 g
Carbohydrates   5.3g
Protein   4.7 g
Cholesterol   25 mg
Sodium   680 mg

Ingredients

1 C. chopped green onions
1 C. chopped spinach
1/2 C. chopped fresh basil
1/2 C. chopped parsley
5 C. chicken broth
1 tsp white sugar

1 C. half-and-half cream
Salt to taste
Ground black pepper to taste
2 tbsp butter
2 tbsp all-purpose flour

Directions

1. Place a large pot over medium heat. Add 3 tbsp of butter and cook it until it melts. Add the onion and cook it for 12 min.
2. Stir in the spinach, basil or watercress, and parsley. Lower the heat and put on the lid. Cook the soup for 12 min.
3. Add the sugar with broth. Put on the lid and cook the soup for 32 min. add the cream gradually while stirring the soup all the time.
4. Place a small saucepan over medium heat. Cook in it 2 tbsp of butter until it melts. Add the flour and cook it for 2 min while mixing all the time.
5. Add some of the hot soup to the pan and stir it until the mix becomes smooth. Transfer the mix to the soup and stir it until it starts boiling.
6. Adjust the seasoning of the soup then serve it warm.
7. Enjoy.

Chicken Flavored Broccoli Soup

🥣 Prep Time: 20 mins
🕐 Total Time: 1 hr 5 mins

Servings per Recipe: 6
Calories	247 kcal
Fat	16.3 g
Carbohydrates	20.2g
Protein	7.5 g
Cholesterol	48 mg
Sodium	1721 mg

Ingredients

- 3 tbsp butter
- 1 onion, chopped
- 4 large carrots, chopped
- 1 clove garlic, chopped
- 4 C. water
- 4 tbsp chicken bouillon powder
- 1 lb fresh broccoli florets
- 2 C. half-and-half
- 3 tbsp all-purpose flour
- 1/4 C. ice water
- 1 tbsp soy sauce
- 1/2 tsp ground black pepper
- 1/4 C. chopped parsley

Directions

1. Place a large saucepan over medium heat. Cook in it the butter until it melts. Stir in the onions, carrots, and garlic. Cook them for 6 in. Reserve 1/2 C. of broccoli florets.
2. Combine 4 C. water and chicken bouillon granules in a large pot. Cook them until they start boiling. Add the cooked onion mix with broccoli florets.
3. Lower the heat and put on the lid. Cook the soup for 18 min.
4. Get a food processor: Allow the soup to cool down for 10 min. blend the soup in batches in the food processor with the remaining broccoli and half and half cream until it becomes smooth and creamy.
5. Pour the soup back into the pot. Cook the soup until it starts boiling. Mix 1/4 C. of water with flour in a small bowl. Stir it into the soup while boiling and cook it until it thickens.
6. Stir in the soy sauce with a pinch of salt and pepper. Adjust the seasoning of the soup then serve it warm.
7. Enjoy.

CHILLED SUMMER
Mango Soup

Prep Time: 10 mins
Total Time: 10 mins

Servings per Recipe: 3
Calories   319 kcal
Fat   14.4 g
Carbohydrates   49.2g
Protein   4.7 g
Cholesterol   45 mg
Sodium   53 mg

Ingredients

2 mango - peeled, seeded, and cubed
1/4 C. white sugar
1 lemon, zested and juiced
1 1/2 C. half-and-half

Directions

1. Get a blender: Combine all the
2. Ingredients in it and blend them smooth.
3. Chill the soup in the fridge until ready to serve.
4. Enjoy.

Italian Basil Tomato Soup

Prep Time: 10 mins
Total Time: 25 mins

Servings per Recipe: 4
Calories   251 kcal
Fat   9.6 g
Carbohydrates   26.1g
Protein   11.6 g
Cholesterol   38 mg
Sodium   1148 mg

Ingredients

1 (26 oz) can tomato soup
2 (14.5 oz) cans Italian-style diced tomatoes, undrained
1/2 C. water
1 C. milk
4 oz crumbled Gorgonzola cheese
2 tbsp minced garlic
1 tbsp dried basil
1 tsp onion powder

Directions

1. Place a large saucepan over medium heat. Stir in all the
2. Ingredients put on the lid and lower the heat. Cook the soup for 18 min.
3. Adjust the seasoning of the soup then serve it warm.
4. Enjoy.

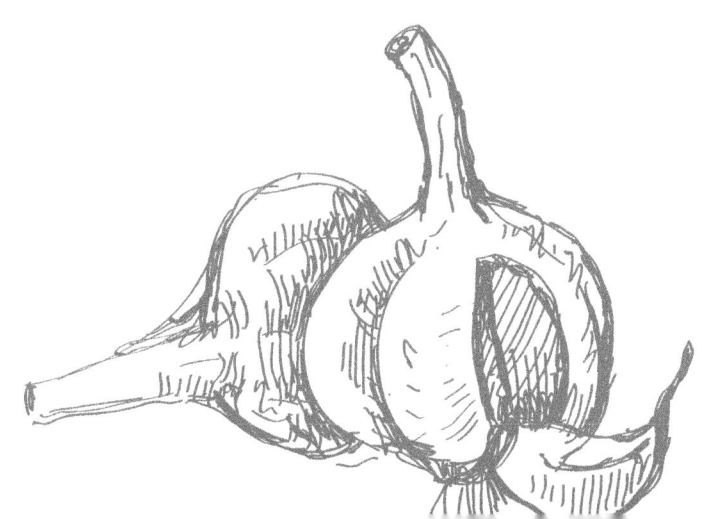

FANCY
Artichoke Soup

🍲 Prep Time: 10 mins
🕐 Total Time: 25 mins

Servings per Recipe: 4
Calories	410 kcal
Fat	24.6 g
Carbohydrates	33.8g
Protein	10 g
Cholesterol	92 mg
Sodium	735 mg

Ingredients

- 4 whole artichokes
- 2 C. water
- 2 C. chicken stock
- 1/2 C. vegetable broth
- 1 potato, diced
- 1 small carrot, diced
- 1 onion, chopped
- 1 small stalk celery, diced
- 2 cloves garlic, minced
- 2 bay leaves
- 1/2 tsp dried marjoram
- 1 C. heavy whipping cream
- 4 tbsp grated Romano cheese
- Salt to taste
- Ground black pepper to taste

Directions

1. Bring 2 C. of water in a large saucepan and bring it to a boil. Place a steamer on it and cook in it the artichokes for 46 min.
2. Place the artichokes aside to lose heat. Reserve the cooking water of the artichokes. Cut the artichoke hearts into dices.
3. Place a large pot over medium heat. Stir in the artichoke heart dices with chicken stock, broth, potato, carrot, onion, celery, garlic, bay leaves, and marjoram.
4. Lower the heat and cook the soup for 47 min.
5. Get a food processor: Allow the soup to cool down for 10 min. blend the soup in batches in the food processor until it becomes smooth and creamy.
6. Pour the soup back into the pot with cheese and cream. Adjust the seasoning of the soup then serve it warm.
7. Enjoy.

Bell Cheese Soup

Prep Time: 25 mins
Total Time: 55 mins

Servings per Recipe: 4
Calories 395 kcal
Fat 33.5 g
Carbohydrates 10.5g
Protein 14.1 g
Cholesterol 108 mg
Sodium 1155 mg

Ingredients

- 1 (26 oz) can tomato soup
- 2 (14.5 oz) cans Italian-style diced tomatoes, undrained
- 1/2 C. water
- 1 C. milk
- 4 oz crumbled Gorgonzola cheese
- 2 tbsp minced garlic
- 1 tbsp dried basil
- 1 tsp onion powder

Directions

1. Place a large saucepan over medium heat. Add the butter and cook it until it melts. Sauté in it the celery with onion for 6 min
2. Add the flour and cook them for 4 min. Add the stock gradually while mixing them gently all the time. Lower the heat and cook the soup for 22 min.
3. Add the brie cheese and stir it gently until it melts for 6 min.
4. Get a food processor: Allow the soup to cool down for 10 min. blend the soup in batches in the food processor until it becomes smooth and creamy.
5. Pour the soup back into the pot. Cook the soup until it starts simmering. Stir in the cream. Adjust the seasoning of the soup then serve it warm.
6. Enjoy.

ROASTED HALLOWEEN
Soup

Prep Time: 10 mins
Total Time: 2 hrs 25 mins

Servings per Recipe: 6
Calories	294 kcal
Fat	5.4 g
Carbohydrates	55.9 g
Protein	6.5 g
Cholesterol	21 mg
Sodium	420 mg

Ingredients

- 3 large sweet potatoes
- 3 (14 oz) cans low-sodium chicken broth
- 1/4 C. brown sugar, or more to taste
- 1/2 tsp salt (to taste)
- 1/4 tsp ground allspice
- Black pepper to taste
- Cayenne pepper to taste
- 1/3 C. heavy cream

Directions

1. Before you do anything set the oven to 350 F.
2. Place the sweet potatoes on a lined up baking sheet. Cook them in the oven for 1 h 30 min. Allow the sweet potato to lose heat for 15 min. Peel the potatoes.
3. Get a food processor: Place the sweet potatoes in the food processor and blend it smooth while adding the broth gradually until it becomes smooth and creamy.
4. Pour the purée in a large pot. Bring the purée to a boil. Lower the heat and add the sugar, salt, allspice, black pepper, and cayenne pepper.
5. Put on the lid and cook the soup for 12 min. Turn off the heat and add the cream. Adjust the seasoning of the soup then serve it warm.
6. Enjoy.

Cheesy Turkey Soup

🥣 Prep Time: 10 mins
🕐 Total Time: 20 mins

Servings per Recipe: 8
Calories   235 kcal
Fat   11.2 g
Carbohydrates   21.3g
Protein   12 g
Cholesterol   35 mg
Sodium   819 mg

Ingredients

- 2 C. milk, or as needed
- 4 C. leftover mashed potatoes
- 2 C. cubed fully cooked turkey
- Salt and ground black pepper to taste
- 1/2 C. shredded Cheddar cheese, or to taste

Directions

1. Pour the milk in a large pot. Cook it over medium heat until it becomes warm. Add the potato and stir them until they become creamy while adding more milk if the mix is too thick.
2. Stir in the turkey and cook the soup for 8 min. Stir in the cheese with a pinch of salt and pepper. Adjust the seasoning of the soup then serve it warm.
3. Enjoy.

CHEESY GREEN
Florets Soup

🥣 Prep Time: 15 mins
🕐 Total Time: 40 mins

Servings per Recipe: 6
Calories   205 kcal
Fat   11.4 g
Carbohydrates   17.2g
Protein   9.7 g
Cholesterol   23 mg
Sodium   901 mg

Ingredients

4 C. water
4 C. broccoli florets
2 tbsp margarine
1 onion, chopped
1 large stalk celery, chopped
1/3 C. all-purpose flour

2 tbsp chicken bouillon powder
2 1/2 C. whole milk
1/4 tsp ground allspice
1/4 tsp ground black pepper
1/2 C. shredded sharp Cheddar cheese

Directions

1. Place a medium pot over medium heat. Add the broccoli with water and cook them until they start boiling. Lower the heat and cook it for 4 min.
2. Remove the broccoli from the water and place it aside to drain. Reserve the cooking water.
3. Get a food processor: Add half of the broccoli then process it until it become smooth. Finely chop the rest of the cooked broccoli and place it aside.
4. Place a medium pot over medium heat. Add the butter and cook it until it melts. Sauté in it the onion with celery for 5 min
5. Add the flour and cook them for 3 min while stirring all the time. Stir in the reserved water and chicken bouillon granules. Cook the soup until it starts boiling while stirring it all the time.
6. Lower the heat and cook the soup for 10 to 14 or until it becomes thick. Add the chopped and puréed broccoli with milk, allspice, salt, and pepper. Cook the soup for 5 min.
7. Adjust the seasoning of the soup then serve it warm.
8. Enjoy.

Spicy Loaded Elk Soup

> Prep Time: 40 mins
> Total Time: 1 hr 40 mins

Servings per Recipe: 8
Calories	196 kcal
Fat	6.6 g
Carbohydrates	22g
Protein	13.8 g
Cholesterol	26 mg
Sodium	323 mg

Ingredients

- 1 lb elk breakfast sausage
- 2 tbsp olive oil
- 3 cloves garlic, minced
- 2 tsp minced fresh ginger root
- 1 onion, chopped
- 2 C. cubed butternut squash
- 2 beets, sliced into rounds
- 4 red potatoes, diced
- 4 carrots, chopped
- 1/2 medium head green cabbage, chopped
- 1 tsp hot pepper sauce (such as Tabasco(R)), or to taste
- 2 tsp dried dill weed
- 2 tsp dried rubbed sage
- 2 tsp dried thyme leaves
- Salt and black pepper to taste
- 2 quarts chicken broth
- 1 (10.75 oz) can condensed cream of mushroom soup
- 1/4 C. red vinegar

Directions

1. Place a large pot over medium heat. Brown in it the sausages for 8 min. Drain the sausages and place them aside. Discard the remaining grease.
2. Heat the olive oil in the same pot. Sauté in it the garlic, ginger, onion, butternut squash, beets, red potatoes, carrots, and cabbage for 10 min
3. Add the hot pepper sauce, dill, sage, thyme, salt, and pepper, sausage, chicken broth, cream of mushroom soup, and vinegar. Cook the soup until it starts simmering.
4. Lower the heat and coo the soup for 34 min with the half lid. Adjust the seasoning of the soup then serve it warm.
5. Enjoy.

CREAMY GORGONZOLA Soup

Prep Time: 10 mins
Total Time: 45 mins

Servings per Recipe: 6
Calories   242 kcal
Fat   18.6 g
Carbohydrates   11.5g
Protein   8.5 g
Cholesterol   30 mg
Sodium   418 mg

Ingredients

2 tbsp olive oil
1 tbsp vegan margarine
1 onion, chopped
2 lb zucchini, sliced
1 tsp dried oregano
Salt and pepper to taste

2 1/2 tsp vegetable bouillon powder
2 1/2 C. water
6 oz crumbled Gorgonzola cheese
1 C. non-dairy creamer

Directions

1. Place a large pot over medium heat. Cook in it the margarine with oil until they melt. Add the onion and cook it for 6 min.
2. Stir in the oregano with zucchini, a pinch of salt and pepper. Cook them for 12 min. Stir in the bouillon powder with water. Cook them until they start boiling.
3. Lower the heat and cook the soup for 12 min. stir in the gorgonzola cheese until it melts completely for 5 min.
4. Get a food processor: Allow the soup to cool down for 10 min. blend the soup in batches in the food processor until it becomes smooth and creamy.
5. Pour the soup back into the pot. Add to it the creamer and heat the soup through. Adjust the seasoning of the soup then serve it warm.
6. Enjoy.

Dill Soup

Prep Time: 10 mins
Total Time: 25 mins

Servings per Recipe: 4
Calories	150 kcal
Fat	13.9 g
Carbohydrates	5.2g
Protein	1.8 g
Cholesterol	40 mg
Sodium	155 mg

Ingredients

- 3 tbsp butter, divided
- 1 small white onion, diced
- 1 dill pickle, diced
- 2 C. water
- 1/2 C. dill pickle juice
- 1 sprig fresh dill, roughly chopped
- 3/4 C. half-and-half
- 1/8 tsp celery salt
- 1 tbsp all-purpose flour

Directions

1. Place a medium pot over medium heat. Add the oil and heat it. Cook in it the dill pickle with onion for 8 min. Stir in the water and cook the soup until it starts boiling.
2. Get a food processor: Allow the soup to cool down for 10 min. blend the soup in batches in the food processor with the half and half cream until it becomes smooth and creamy.
3. Pour the soup back into the pot. Add to it the celery salt and cook it until it starts simmering. Melt the butter in a small pan. Add to it the flour and mix them for 6 min on low heat.
4. Transfer the mix to the soup and stir it on low heat until it thickens. Adjust the seasoning of the soup then serve it warm.
5. Enjoy.

CREAMY MASALA
Quinoa Soup

🥣 Prep Time: 25 mins
🕐 Total Time: 1 hr 10 mins

Servings per Recipe: 4
Calories	405 kcal
Fat	13.3 g
Carbohydrates	60.9g
Protein	13.8 g
Cholesterol	0 mg
Sodium	579 mg

Ingredients

- 2 C. water
- 1 C. quinoa, or more to taste
- 1 tbsp vegetable oil
- 1 large onion, chopped
- 4 C. homemade vegetable stock
- 4 C. chopped broccoli
- 1 sweet potato, peeled and cut into 1-inch pieces
- Salt to taste
- 1 pinch ground allspice, or to taste
- 1 pinch garam masala, or to taste
- 1 pinch ground pepper to taste

Cashew Cream:
- 1/2 C. water (optional)
- 2 oz raw cashews (optional)

Directions

1. Pour 2 C. of water in a large saucepan. Add to it the quinoa and cook it until it starts boiling. Lower the heat and cook the quinoa for 18 min.
2. Place medium heavy pot over medium heat. Add the oil and heat it. Cook in it the onion for 6 min. add the stock, broccoli, sweet potato, and salt.
3. Cook the soup until it starts boiling. Lower the heat and cook the soup for 18 min. turn off the heat. Stir in the allspice, garam masala, and pepper.
4. Get a food processor: Allow the soup to cool down for 10 min. blend the soup in batches in the food processor until it becomes smooth and creamy. Pour the soup back into the pot.
5. Get a blender: Combine the water with cashews and blend them until they become creamy. Stir the mix into the soup. Bring the soup to a boil.
6. Adjust the seasoning of the soup then serve it warm over the quinoa.
7. Enjoy.

Creamy Pumpkin
Asiago Soup

🥣 Prep Time: 30 mins
🕐 Total Time: 1 hr 30 mins

Servings per Recipe: 12
Calories   275 kcal
Fat   16.6 g
Carbohydrates   28.4g
Protein   7.3 g
Cholesterol   52 mg
Sodium   820 mg

Ingredients

- 6 C. cubed butternut squash
- 2 tbsp butter
- 3 carrots, chopped
- 1 large onion, chopped
- 1 C. chopped celery
- 1 C. heavy cream
- 1 C. sour cream
- 8 C. chicken broth
- 1 tsp ground allspice
- 1 tsp ground black pepper
- Salt to taste
- 6 small sugar pumpkins, halved and seeded
- 1 C. grated Asiago cheese, divided

Directions

1. Place a large saucepan over medium heat. Add the butternut squash dices and cover them with water. Cook them until they start boiling.
2. Cook the butternut squash for 35 min. Drain it and discard the water.
3. Before you do anything set the oven to 350 F. Grease a baking pan with some oil.
4. Place a large skillet over medium heat. Add the butter and cook it until it melts. Sauté in it the carrots, onion, and celery for 12 min
5. Get a blender: Transfer the cooked veggies with butternut squash, sour cream and cream to it. Blend them smooth. Pour the mix into back into the pot.
6. Add to it the chicken broth, allspice, black pepper, and salt. Cook them until they start boiling. Lower the heat and cook the soup for 16 min.
7. Place the pumpkin halves on the baking pan with the open side facing up. Cook it in the oven for 18 min.
8. Preheat the broiler. Broil the pumpkin halves until they become browned. Spoon the hot soup into the pumpkin halves then serve them right away.
9. Enjoy.

CLASSIC CREAMY
Potato Soup

Prep Time: 15 mins
Total Time: 45 mins

Servings per Recipe: 2
Calories	453 kcal
Fat	35 g
Carbohydrates	28.2g
Protein	9.8 g
Cholesterol	112 mg
Sodium	1004 mg

Ingredients

2 tbsp butter
1 onion, thinly sliced
1 small potatoes, thinly sliced
2 C. fresh chopped broccoli
1 1/2 C. chicken broth

1/4 tsp salt
Ground black pepper to taste
1/2 C. heavy whipping cream

Directions

1. Place a small saucepan over medium heat. Melt the butter in it. Add the potato with broccoli and onion. Put on the lid and cook them for 4 min.
2. Stir in the stock. Cook the soup until it starts boiling. Cook the soup for 15 to 20 min or until the veggies become tender.
3. Get a food processor: Allow the soup to cool down for 10 min. blend the soup in batches in the food processor until it becomes smooth and creamy. Pour the soup back into the pot.
4. Stir in the cream with a pinch of salt and pepper. Cook the soup for 2 min to heat it. Adjust the seasoning of the soup then serve it warm.
5. Enjoy.

Chunky Chicken and Lemon Soup

Prep Time: 10 mins
Total Time: 30 mins

Servings per Recipe: 15
Calories 323 kcal
Fat 13.5 g
Carbohydrates 23.8g
Protein 24.4 g
Cholesterol 69 mg
Sodium 2011 mg

Ingredients

2 (48 oz) containers chicken broth
4 (12 oz) cans chicken chunks, drained
1 1/2 C. white rice

2 (26 oz) cans cream of chicken soup
3/4 cup .lemon juice, or to taste

Directions

1. Place a large pot over medium heat. Add the chicken with broth and cook them until they start boiling. Stir in the rice. Cook the soup for 18 min.
2. Add the cream of chicken soup with lemon juice. Cook the soup for 8 min while stirring all the time. Adjust the seasoning of the soup then serve it hot.
3. Enjoy.

WORCESTERSHIRE
Cheddar Soup

Prep Time: 15 mins
Total Time: 1 hr

Servings per Recipe: 8
Calories   339 kcal
Fat   30.2 g
Carbohydrates   11.9 g
Protein   7.4 g
Cholesterol   105 mg
Sodium   787 mg

Ingredients

2 tbsp butter
1/2 large onion, diced
1 clove garlic, minced
1 tbsp all-purpose flour
6 C. chicken stock, divided
2 C. chopped fiddlehead ferns
1 carrot, diced
1 potato, diced

2 C. heavy whipping cream
1 tbsp Worcestershire sauce (optional)
1 tbsp soy sauce (optional)
Salt and ground black pepper to taste
1 C. shredded Cheddar cheese (optional)

Directions

1. Place a large soup pot over medium heat. Add the butter and cook it until it melts. Sauté in it the garlic with onion for 6 min
2. Add the flour and cook them for 3 min. Stir in the stock and cook the soup until it starts boiling. Add the fiddleheads, carrot, and potato.
3. Lower the heat and put on the lid. Cook the soup for 35 min.
4. Get a food processor: Allow the soup to cool down for 10 min. blend the soup in batches in the food processor until it becomes smooth and creamy. Pour the soup back into the pot.
5. Stir in the cream with a pinch of salt and pepper. Cook the soup for 5 min to heat it. Add the Worcestershire sauce and soy sauce.
6. Adjust the seasoning of the soup then serve it warm.
7. Enjoy.

Creamy Bacon Soup

Prep Time: 10 mins
Total Time: 45 mins

Servings per Recipe: 2
Calories	188 kcal
Fat	5.3 g
Carbohydrates	26.5g
Protein	9.6 g
Cholesterol	15 mg
Sodium	325 mg

Ingredients

- 2 slices turkey bacon, chopped
- 1 C. peeled and cubed potatoes
- 1/3 C. chopped onion
- 1 C. chopped assorted mushrooms
- 1 tsp garlic powder
- 1/2 tsp onion powder
- 1 1/2 C. water
- 1/2 C. milk
- 1 sprig fresh thyme
- 1 1/2 tbsp all-purpose flour
- Salt and coarsely ground black pepper to taste

Directions

1. Cook the bacon in a large pot until it becomes crispy. Add the potato with onion and cook them for 6 min.
2. Stir in the mushrooms, garlic powder, and onion powder. Cook them for 6 min. Stir in the water with milk, flour, thyme, salt and pepper.
3. Cook the soup until it starts boiling. Keep the soup boiling for 18 to 20 min or until the potato becomes soft while adding more broth if needed.
4. Mash some of the potato in the soup to make it chunky. Adjust the seasoning of the soup then serve it warm.
5. Enjoy.

CHILLED CREAMY
Dill Soup

Prep Time: 15 mins
Total Time: 1 hr 45 mins

Servings per Recipe: 8
Calories	171 kcal
Fat	15.1 g
Carbohydrates	8.4g
Protein	2.3 g
Cholesterol	41 mg
Sodium	408 mg

Ingredients

2 tbsp vegetable oil
1 large sweet onion, peeled and chopped
6 large cucumbers - peeled, seeded, and cut into pieces
4 C. chicken stock
2 tbsp dill weed
Salt and ground black pepper to taste
1 C. heavy whipping cream

Directions

1. Place a large soup pot over medium heat. Heat the oil in it. Sauté in it the onion for 9 min
2. Add the cucumbers, chicken broth, dill weed, salt, and pepper. Lower the heat and put on the lid. Cook the soup for 22 min.
3. Get a food processor: Allow the soup to cool down for 10 min. blend the soup in batches in the food processor until it becomes smooth and creamy. Pour the soup back into the pot.
4. Stir in the cream with a pinch of salt and pepper. Place the soup in the fridge to lose heat for 1 h then serve it.
5. Enjoy.

Limy Corn Soup

Prep Time: 20 mins
Total Time: 2 hrs 40 mins

Servings per Recipe: 10
Calories   312 kcal
Fat   10.2 g
Carbohydrates   47.8g
Protein   9.8 g
Cholesterol   20 mg
Sodium   271 mg

Ingredients

- 1 lb dried baby lima beans
- 4 1/2 C. water
- Salt and pepper to taste
- 1 (15 oz) can whole kernel corn
- 1 (14.5 oz) can peeled and diced tomatoes
- 8 large potatoes, peeled and cubed
- 3 C. shredded cabbage
- 1 (16 oz) container sour cream

Directions

1. Place a large pot over medium heat. Place in it the lima beans with a pinch of salt and pepper then cover it with water. Cook them until they start boiling.
2. Put on the lid and cook them for 1 h 45 min. Stir in the potato with tomato, corn and cabbage. Cook the soup for 22 min.
3. Stir in the cream. Adjust the seasoning of the soup then serve it warm.
4. Enjoy.

FANCY ASPARAGUS
Cream

🍲 Prep Time: 10 mins
🕐 Total Time: 50 mins

Servings per Recipe: 8
Calories	112 kcal
Fat	8.1 g
Carbohydrates	6.3g
Protein	4.3 g
Cholesterol	6 mg
Sodium	552 mg

Ingredients

1 lb fresh asparagus
3 1/2 C. chicken broth
1/4 C. margarine
1/4 C. all-purpose flour

1/2 C. half-and-half
1/2 tsp salt
1/8 tsp ground black pepper

Directions

1. Remove the ends of asparagus and cut them into 1 inch each.
2. Place a large skillet over medium heat. Add 1 C. of broth with asparagus. Cook them for 8 min.
3. Place a large saucepan over medium heat. Cook the butter in it until it melts. Stir in the 2 1/2 C. of broth with flour and stir them until they become smooth.
4. Stir in the half and half with asparagus mix, salt and pepper. Mix them well. Adjust the seasoning of the soup then serve it warm.
5. Enjoy.

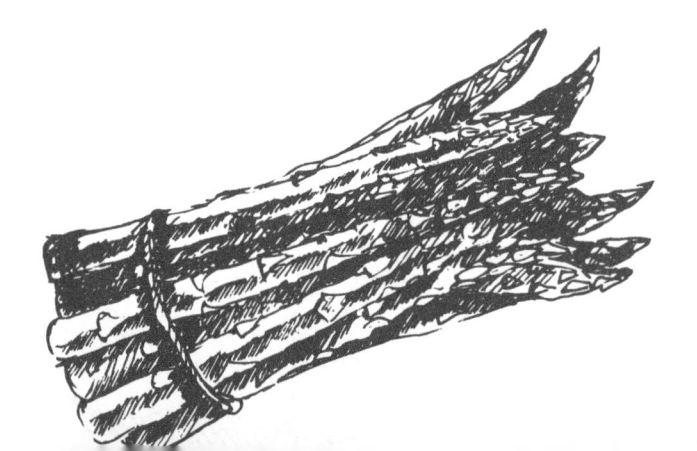

Hot Cheese Soup

Prep Time: 10 mins
Total Time: 25 mins

Servings per Recipe: 6
Calories	186 kcal
Fat	8.3 g
Carbohydrates	17.9 g
Protein	11.4 g
Cholesterol	26 mg
Sodium	529 mg

Ingredients

- 3 C. water
- 2 C. chopped broccoli
- 8 oz mushrooms, sliced
- 2 tbsp butter
- 1 C. nonfat dry milk powder
- 1 (10.75 oz) can condensed Cheddar cheese soup
- 2 dashes hot sauce
- 1/8 tsp ground black pepper
- 1 dash garlic powder

Directions

1. Place a large soup pot over medium heat. Add the water, broccoli, mushrooms, and butter. Cook them until they start boiling. Lower the heat and cook the soup for 6 min.
2. Stir in the remaining
3. Ingredients Cook the soup for 5 min. Adjust the seasoning of the soup then serve it warm.
4. Enjoy.

JERUSALEM CHICKEN
Cream

🥣 Prep Time: 20 mins
⏱ Total Time: 50 mins

Servings per Recipe: 4
Calories	491 kcal
Fat	29.3 g
Carbohydrates	47.2g
Protein	10 g
Cholesterol	92 mg
Sodium	686 mg

Ingredients

- 1/4 C. butter
- 2 onions, minced
- 1 lb Jerusalem artichokes, roughly chopped
- 2 potatoes, peeled and cubed
- 1 tbsp grape juice
- 1 tbsp all-purpose flour
- 3 C. chicken broth
- 3/4 C. heavy whipping cream
- Salt and pepper to taste
- 1/4 C. chopped fresh parsley, for garnish

Directions

1. Place a large skillet over medium heat. Cook in it the butter until it melts. Cook in it the artichoke hearts with potato and onion. Cook them for 12 min.
2. Put on the lid and cook them for 2 min. add the flour with grape juice. Cook them for 2 min. Stir in 2 C. of broth.
3. Cook the soup until it starts boiling while stirring it all the time. Lower the heat and cook the soup for 6 min.
4. Get a food processor: Allow the soup to cool down for 10 min. blend the soup in batches in the food processor until it becomes smooth and creamy. Pour the soup back into the pot.
5. Stir in the cream with a pinch of salt and pepper. Serve your soup warm.
6. Enjoy.

Chunky Milk Soup

Prep Time: 20 mins
Total Time: 1 hr 30 mins

Servings per Recipe: 10
Calories   940 kcal
Fat   82.6 g
Carbohydrates   32.3g
Protein   20.9 g
Cholesterol   319 mg
Sodium   681 mg

Ingredients

- 1/2 C. butter
- 1/2 C. all-purpose flour
- 1 onion, chopped
- 1 bunch chopped fresh chives
- 2 quarts heavy cream
- 2 C. water
- 1 quart milk
- 3 tsp ground cumin
- 2 tsp salt
- 2 tsp ground black pepper
- 2 tsp garlic powder
- 2 tsp dried thyme
- 4 potatoes, peeled and cubed
- 1 lb skinless, boneless chicken breast halves - cut into cubes
- 3 tbsp chopped fresh parsley

Directions

1. Place a large pot over medium heat. Cook in it the butter until it melts. Add the flour and stir it for 1 min.
2. Add the onion with chives and cook them for 6 min. Stir in the cream, water, milk, cumin, salt, ground black pepper, garlic powder, thyme, potatoes and chicken.
3. Lower the heat and cook the soup for 65 min. Place the soup aside to lose heat for 10 min. serve your soup hot.
4. Enjoy.

HERBED CHICKEN
Soup

Prep Time: 15 mins
Total Time: 30 mins

Servings per Recipe: 4
Calories	243 kcal
Fat	4.8 g
Carbohydrates	42.2g
Protein	8.4 g
Cholesterol	13 mg
Sodium	397 mg

Ingredients

- 4 potatoes - peeled and cubed
- 1 1/2 C. chicken broth
- 1 tbsp unsalted butter
- 1/8 tsp salt
- Ground black pepper to taste
- 1 tbsp chopped onion
- 1/8 tsp dried dill weed
- 1 tbsp all-purpose flour
- 1 C. milk

Directions

1. Place a medium pot over medium heat. Pour in it the broth with potato and cook them for 16 min. drain the potatoes.
2. Get a food processor: Place 3/4 C. of the broth with the potatoes and blend them smooth. Pour in the rest of the broth and blend them again.
3. Place a medium saucepan over medium heat. Cook in it the butter until it melts. Add the onion with dill, a pinch of salt and pepper. Cook them for 3 min.
4. Add the flour and cook them for 1 min. Stir in the milk and cook them for 2 min. add the potato mix.
5. Cook the soup for 5 min to heat it. Adjust the seasoning of the soup then serve it warm.
6. Enjoy.

Apple Cider Beef Soup

Prep Time: 10 mins
Total Time: 30 mins

Servings per Recipe: 8
Calories	208 kcal
Fat	17.4 g
Carbohydrates	9.6g
Protein	3 g
Cholesterol	60 mg
Sodium	955 mg

Ingredients

- 1/4 C. butter
- 1 lb fresh mushrooms, sliced
- 1/4 C. all-purpose flour
- 3 (14 oz) cans chicken broth
- 1 cube beef bouillon
- 1/2 C. apple cider vinegar
- 1 C. heavy cream

Directions

1. Place a large soup pot over medium heat. Add the butter and cook it until it melts. Sauté in it the mushrooms for 6 min. add the flour and cook them for 1 min.
2. Stir in the broth gradually while stirring all the time. Add the beef bouillon with apple cider. Cook the soup until it start boiling.
3. Turn off the heat. Stir in the cream. Cook the soup on low heat for 3 min. serve it hot.
4. Enjoy.

BAKED SPEARS
Soup Casserole

Prep Time: 10 mins
Total Time: 1 hr 05 mins

Servings per Recipe: 5
Calories	279 kcal
Fat	10.6 g
Carbohydrates	15.5g
Protein	28.8 g
Cholesterol	71 mg
Sodium	894 mg

Ingredients

5 skinless, boneless chicken breast halves
20 spears fresh asparagus, trimmed, or as needed
2 (10.75 oz) cans cream of asparagus soup

1 1/2 C. milk
Italian seasoned bread crumbs

Directions

1. Before you do anything set the oven to 350 F. Coat a casserole dish with butter or oil.
2. Season the chicken breasts with some salt and pepper. Place the chicken breasts in the casserole and cook them in the oven for 30 min.
3. In the meantime, bring a salted pot of water to a boil. Cook in it the asparagus for 6 min. Drain the asparagus and discard the water.
4. Get a mixing bowl: Whisk the milk with asparagus soup. Arrange the asparagus spears on the chicken breasts.
5. Pour the soup mix all over them then top them with some seasoned breadcrumbs. Cook the soup the casserole in the oven for 28 min. Serve it hot.
6. Enjoy.

Pesto Topping Soup

Prep Time: 10 mins
Total Time: 30 mins

Servings per Recipe: 6
Calories	125 kcal
Fat	7.9 g
Carbohydrates	9.4g
Protein	4.5 g
Cholesterol	20 mg
Sodium	1210 mg

Ingredients

- 1 (32 fluid oz) container chicken broth
- 1 (14.5 oz) can diced tomatoes with juice
- 1 (14.5 oz) can diced tomatoes with garlic and onion
- 1 C. half-and-half cream
- Salt and pepper to taste
- 2 tbsp basil pesto

Directions

1. Place a large soup pot over medium heat. Pour in it the broth and cook it until it starts boiling. Lower the heat and keep it boiling until it reduces by 1/3.
2. Stir in the canned tomato. Bring the soup to a simmer. Stir in the half and half. Lower the heat. Cook the soup for 16 min.
3. Get a food processor: Allow the soup to cool down for 10 min. blend the soup in batches in the food processor until it becomes smooth and creamy. Pour the soup back into the pot.
4. Stir in the cream with a pinch of salt and pepper. Serve your soup warm with the pesto as a topping.
5. Enjoy.

OLD BAY'S CREAMY
Crab Soup

🥣 Prep Time: 15 mins
🕐 Total Time: 45 mins

Servings per Recipe: 8
Calories   383 kcal
Fat   27.1 g
Carbohydrates   15.9 g
Protein   19.5 g
Cholesterol   128 mg
Sodium   1896 mg

Ingredients

1/2 C. butter
1 onion, chopped
3 celery, chopped
3 tbsp all-purpose flour
4 C. water
1 (10.5 oz) can condensed chicken broth
4 tbsp chicken soup base
1 tbsp chopped fresh parsley
1 potato, peeled and diced
1 quart half-and-half cream
1 tbsp soy sauce
1 lb crabmeat
1 tsp Old Bay Seasoning TM
Salt and pepper to taste

Directions

1. Place a large soup pot over medium heat. Cook in it the butter until it melts. Add the celery with onion and cook them for 5 min.
2. Add the flour and stir them for 2 min. Stir in the broth with chicken soup base and broth until they are well combined. Cook the soup until it starts boiling.
3. Add the potato with parsley. Lower the heat and cook the soup for 22 min. Add the rest of the
4. Ingredients
5. Change the heat to medium. Cook the soup until it starts boiling. Adjust the seasoning of the soup then serve it warm.
6. Enjoy.

Anti-Vampires Soup

🍲 Prep Time: 15 mins
🕐 Total Time: 1 hr 25 mins

Servings per Recipe: 5
Calories   399 kcal
Fat   28.9 g
Carbohydrates   18.2g
Protein   9.1 g
Cholesterol   75 mg
Sodium   457 mg

Ingredients

- 3/4 C. garlic cloves, peeled
- 3 tbsp olive oil
- 2 1/2 C. chicken broth
- 1 C. vegetable broth
- 2 1/2 C. milk
- 1 C. heavy whipping cream
- 1/2 C. peeled and cubed potatoes
- Salt and pepper to taste

Directions

1. Get a food processor: Add the garlic and pulse it several times until it becomes like a paste.
2. Place a large saucepan over low heat. Cook in it the garlic for 2 min while stirring it often. Add the broth then cook them until they start boiling.
3. Lower the heat and cook the soup for 34 min. add the potato with cream and milk. Cook the soup for 34 min.
4. Get a food processor: Blend the soup in batches until it becomes smooth and creamy. Pour the soup back into the pot.
5. Cook the soup until it starts simmering. Adjust the seasoning of the soup then serve it warm.
6. Enjoy.

CHEESY PARSLEY
Flowers Soup

Prep Time: 15 mins
Total Time: 1 hr

Servings per Recipe: 6
Calories   238 kcal
Fat   14.5 g
Carbohydrates   20.4g
Protein   7.8 g
Cholesterol   41 mg
Sodium   1031 mg

Ingredients

- 1 head cauliflower, chopped
- 1 tbsp vegetable oil
- 1 yellow onion, chopped
- 2 cloves garlic, chopped
- 1 leek, chopped
- 3 stalks celery, chopped
- 1 baking potato, thinly sliced
- 2 C. chicken broth
- 1/4 C. apple cider
- 1 tsp white pepper
- 1 tsp black pepper
- 1/2 C. milk
- 1 tsp salt
- 1/2 C. heavy cream
- 3 oz Stilton cheese
- 1/4 C. chopped fresh parsley

Directions

1. Bring a salted pot of water to a boil. Cook in it 3/4 C. of the cauliflower florets for 4 min. Rinse it with cold water and place it aside.
2. Place a large pot over medium heat. Heat the oil in it. Cook in it the onion, garlic, leek and celery for 6 min. Stir in the potato, chicken broth, raw cauliflower and apple cider.
3. Cook the soup until starts boiling. Lower the heat and cook the soup for 18 to 20 min while stirring it from time to time.
4. Turn off the heat and allow the soup to cool down for 10 min.
5. Get a food processor: Blend the soup in batches until it becomes smooth and creamy. Pour the soup back into the pot. Stir in the cheese with cream and milk.
6. Cook the soup on low heat for 5 min. Adjust the seasoning of the soup then serve it warm with 3/4 C. of cooked cauliflower florets and parsley.
7. Enjoy.

Alaskan Broth Soup

Prep Time: 10 mins
Total Time: 1 hr 05 mins

Servings per Recipe: 4
Calories   329 kcal
Fat   11.2 g
Carbohydrates   38.3g
Protein   6.1 g
Cholesterol   3 mg
Sodium   < 1086 mg

Ingredients

- 2 C. thinly sliced carrots
- 1/2 C. chopped onion
- 1/2 C. fish broth
- 1/2 C. water
- 3 cubes chicken bouillon
- 4 tbsp margarine
- 2 C. skim milk
- 2 tbsp all-purpose flour
- 2 tbsp white sugar
- 1/4 tsp ground ginger
- 3 tbsp chopped fresh parsley
- Salt to taste
- Ground black pepper to taste

Directions

1. Place a medium pot over medium heat. Add the carrots, onions, water, chicken bouillon cubes, and margarine.
2. Bring the soup to a simmer. Cook the soup for 15 min. Place it aside to lose heat for 10 min.
3. Get a food processor: Blend the soup with milk, flour, sugar, and ground ginger until it becomes smooth and creamy. Pour the soup back into the pot.
4. Cook the soup on low heat for 6 min until it thickens. Adjust the seasoning of the soup then serve it warm.
5. Enjoy.

TWISTED ONION Soup

🥣 Prep Time: 10 mins
🕐 Total Time: 1 hr 05 mins

Servings per Recipe: 24
Calories   182 kcal
Fat   4.9 g
Carbohydrates   29.5g
Protein   6 g
Cholesterol   15 mg
Sodium   67 mg

Ingredients

12 potatoes, peeled and cubed
12 onions, chopped
6 tbsp all-purpose flour
6 tbsp butter

9 C. milk
3 tbsp chopped fresh parsley
Salt and pepper to taste

Directions

1. Place a large soup pot over medium heat. Add the onion with potato then cover them with water. Cook them until they start boiling. Keep boiling them for 40 min.
2. Remove the potatoes and onion from the water. Place 3 C. of the cooking water aside.
3. Get a food processor: Blend the potato and onion with the reserved water in batches until they become smooth and creamy. Pour the soup back into the pot.
4. Place a medium saucepan over medium heat. Cook in it the butter until it melts. Add the flour and stir it for 1 min. Add the milk gradually while whisking them all the time.
5. Lower the heat and stir in the onion mix. Cook the soup until it starts simmer. Keep simmering it for 8 min while stirring often.
6. Stir in the parsley. Adjust the seasoning of the soup then serve it hot.
7. Enjoy.

Creamy Mozzarella Soup

🥣 Prep Time: 30 mins
⏲ Total Time: 1 hr 30 mins

Servings per Recipe: 15
Calories   443 kcal
Fat   36.9 g
Carbohydrates   17g
Protein   13.5 g
Cholesterol   128 mg
Sodium   1488 mg

Ingredients

- 1 head fresh broccoli
- 3 tbsp butter
- 3 tbsp minced onion
- 1 stalk celery with leaves, chopped
- 3 tbsp all-purpose flour
- 1 C. milk
- 1 C. heavy cream
- 2 cubes chicken bouillon
- 1 tsp Worcestershire sauce
- 2 pinches paprika
- 1 tsp salt
- 1 C. shredded mozzarella cheese

Directions

1. Bring a salted pot of water to a boil. Add the broccoli and cook them until they start boiling. Lower the heat and cook it for 16 min.
2. Drain the broccoli from the water and place it aside. Place 2 C. of the cooking water aside.
3. Place a large saucepan over medium heat. Cook in it the butter until it melts. Add the celery with onion and cook them for 14 min.
4. Add the milk with cream and flour then stir them. Stir the 2 C. of the broccoli's reserved cooking water with bouillon until it dissolves completely.
5. Add the Worcestershire, cheese, paprika and salt. Cook the soup for 12 min while stirring it often until the cheese melts.
6. Adjust the seasoning of the soup then serve it hot.
7. Enjoy.

CLASSIC TOMATO
Soup

🍲 Prep Time: 5 mins
🕒 Total Time: 25 mins

Servings per Recipe: 4
Calories   119 kcal
Fat   5.6 g
Carbohydrates   14.3g
Protein   4.4 g
Cholesterol   17 mg
Sodium   494 mg

Ingredients

2 tbsp butter
1 onion, chopped
2 tbsp all-purpose flour
1 quart tomato juice

Salt to taste
2 C. milk

Directions

1. Place a medium pot over medium heat. Cook in it the onion until it melts. Add the onion and cook it for 4 min.
2. Turn of the heat and add the four then mix them well. Add the tomato juice gradually while mixing them all the time. Turn on the heat to medium.
3. Cook the soup until it becomes about to boil. Turn off the heat and allow the soup to lose heat for 12 min. Stir in the milk.
4. Adjust the seasoning of the soup then serve it.
5. Enjoy.

Festive Sweet and Salty Pumpkin Soup

Prep Time: 10 mins
Total Time: 50 mins

Servings per Recipe: 6
Calories   313 kcal
Fat   25.1 g
Carbohydrates   19.6g
Protein   4.5 g
Cholesterol   65 mg
Sodium   769 mg

Ingredients

- 3 tbsp margarine, softened
- 1 tbsp brown sugar
- 1/4 tsp ground cinnamon
- 4 slices whole wheat bread
- 1 C. chopped onion
- 2 tbsp butter, melted
- 2 (14.5 oz) cans chicken broth
- 1 (15 oz) can pumpkin puree
- 1 tsp salt
- 1/4 tsp ground cinnamon
- 1/8 tsp ground ginger
- 1/8 tsp ground black pepper
- 1 C. heavy whipping cream

Directions

1. Before you do anything set the oven to 400 F.
2. Get a small mixing bowl: Mix in it the butter, brown sugar, and cinnamon. Spread the mix on one side of each bread slice.
3. Lay the bread slices with the buttered side facing up on a lined up baking sheet. Cook the bread slices in the oven for 12 min. Cut each bread slices into 8 small squares and place them aside.
4. Place a large pot over medium heat. Add the butter and melt in it. Cook in it the onion for 4 min. Stir in the broth. Cook the soup until it starts boiling.
5. Lower the heat and cook the soup for 18 min. Turn off the heat and allow the soup to cool down for 10 min.
6. Get a food processor: Blend the soup until becomes smooth and creamy. Pour the soup back into the pot.
7. Stir in the rest of the broth, pumpkin, salt, ground cinnamon, ground ginger, and ground pepper. Cook the soup until it starts boiling.
8. Lower the heat and cook it for 12 min. Stir in the cream into the soup. Adjust the seasoning of the soup then serve it warm. Enjoy.

CREAMY SAUSAGE
Mushroom Soup

Prep Time: 15 mins
Total Time: 45 mins

Servings per Recipe: 4
Calories	399 kcal
Fat	22.8 g
Carbohydrates	37.1g
Protein	13.2 g
Cholesterol	56 mg
Sodium	867 mg

Ingredients

- 2 C. chicken broth
- 1 C. water
- 3 potatoes, peeled and chopped
- 1 tbsp vegetable oil, or as needed
- 1 onion, chopped
- 1/2 C. sliced mushrooms
- 1 broccoli stalk, peeled and chopped
- 1/2 C. chopped smoked beef sausage
- 2 cloves garlic, chopped
- 1 C. finely chopped kale
- Salt and ground black pepper to taste
- 1/4 C. heavy whipping cream
- 1/4 C. light cream

Directions

1. Combine the water with broth in a large saucepan. Cook them until they start boiling. Add the potato and cook them for 18 min. Press the potato when it is done with a spoon or fork to mash it.
2. Place a large pan on medium heat. Heat the oil in it. Cook in it the mushroom with broccoli stalk and onion for 8 min.
3. Lower the heat and add the sausage. Cook them for 6 min. add the garlic and cook them for 1 min. Transfer the mix to the pot with the potato mix.
4. Stir in the kale gradually and cook the soup for 5 min until it welts. Lower the heat and add the whipping cream with light cream. Cook the soup for another minute.
5. Adjust the seasoning of the soup then serve it warm.
6. Enjoy.

Homemade Chicken and Mushroom Cream Soup

🥣 Prep Time: 20 mins
🕐 Total Time: 50 mins

Servings per Recipe: 6
Calories   148 kcal
Fat   11 g
Carbohydrates   8.6g
Protein   4.8 g
Cholesterol   30 mg
Sodium   364 mg

Ingredients

5 C. sliced fresh mushrooms
1 1/2 C. chicken broth
1/2 C. chopped onion
1/8 tsp dried thyme
3 tbsp butter
3 tbsp all-purpose flour
1/4 tsp salt

1/4 tsp ground black pepper
1 C. half-and-half
1 tbsp apple cider, optional

Directions

1. Place a large saucepan over medium heat. Add the onion with broth, mushroom and thyme. Cook them for 14 min.
2. Get a food processor: Transfer the mushroom mix to it and pulse them several times until they become finely chopped. Place the mix aside.
3. Place a large saucepan over medium heat. Add the butter on cook it until it melts. Stir flour and mix them. Season them with some salt and pepper.
4. Stir in the half and half and mushroom mix Cook the soup until it starts boiling while stirring all the time until the soup thickens.
5. Check the seasoning of the soup and serve it warm.
6. Enjoy.